A Kid's Guide to Drawing America™

How to Draw
Montana's
Sights and Symbols

Jaycee Kuedee

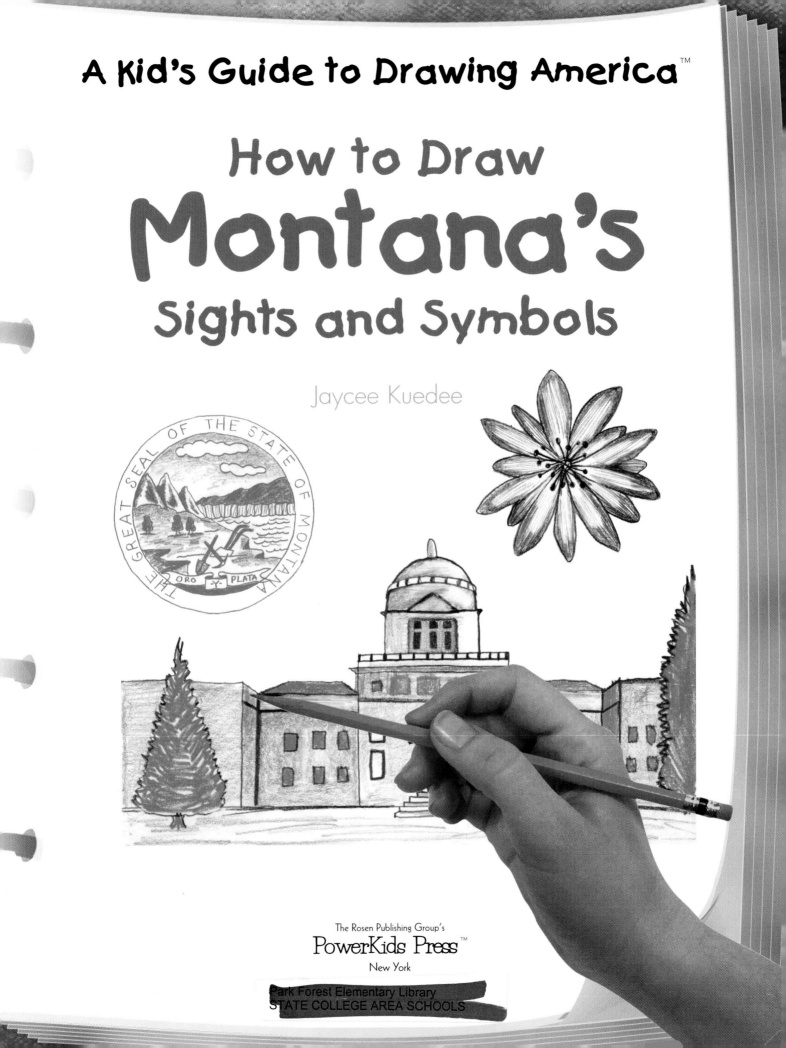

The Rosen Publishing Group's
PowerKids Press™
New York

For Dad, who loves Montana

Published in 2002 by The Rosen Publishing Group, Inc.
29 East 21st Street, New York, NY 10010

First Edition

Book Design: Kim Sonsky
Layout Design: Dean Galiano
Project Editors: Jannell Khu, Jennifer Landau

Illustration Credits: Emily Muschinske
Photo Credits: p. 7 © Neil Rabinowitz/CORBIS; p. 8 (photo and sketch) © courtesy Sid Richardson Collection of Western Art, Fort Worth, Texas; p. 9 © courtesy of the Eiteljorg Museum of American Indians and Western Art; pp. 12, 14 © One Mile Up, Incorporated; pp. 16, 24 © Darrell Gulin/CORBIS; p. 18 © Buddy Mays/CORBIS; p. 20 © Joe McDonald/CORBIS; p. 22 © Carol Cohen/CORBIS; p. 26 © Kennan Ward/CORBIS; p. 28 © Michael Lewis/CORBIS.

Kuedee, Jaycee
        How to draw Montana's sights and symbols / Jaycee Kuedee.
            p. cm. — (A kid's guide to drawing America)
        Includes index.
        Summary: This book explains how to draw some of Montana's sights and symbols, including the state seal, the official flower, and a Rocky Mountain landscape.
        ISBN 0-8239-6082-X
        1. Emblems, State—Montana—Juvenile literature 2. Montana—In art—Juvenile literature
3. Drawing—Technique—Juvenile literature [1. Emblems, State—Montana 2. Montana 3. Drawing—Technique]
I. Title II. Series
        2001
        743'.8'99786—dc21

Manufactured in the United States of America

CONTENTS

Let's Draw Montana

By 1805, Native American groups, like the Blackfeet, had been living for centuries on the land we now call Montana. In that year, Meriwether Lewis and William Clark became the first Europeans to explore the area. The United States had acquired the land from France in 1803, as part of the Louisiana Purchase. This agreement between U.S. president Thomas Jefferson and French ruler Napoleon Bonaparte doubled the size of America. France sold 885,000 square miles (2,292,139 sq km) of land to the United States. In 1864, Montana became a territory. Virginia City was chosen as its capital. During the 1860s, many Americans moved to western territories, such as Montana. The Free Homestead Act of 1862 gave Americans land as long as they lived and worked on it. In 1875, Helena became the territorial capital. On November 8, 1889, Montana became the forty-first state. Five years later, the capital was moved from Virginia City to Helena.

Montana is famous for its huge cattle ranches. Agriculture is the state's number-one industry.

Another important industry is the dairy industry. Other important crops are wheat and hay. Tourism is also a big business in Montana. Thousands of people visit Montana every year to enjoy all that the state has to offer, including its beautiful skies. In fact one of Montana's nicknames is Big Sky Country.

Using this book, you will learn about Montana's sights and symbols and how to draw them. Under every drawing, directions help explain how to do the step. New steps are shown in red to help guide you.

The supplies you will need to draw Montana's sights and symbols are:

- A sketch pad
- An eraser
- A number 2 pencil
- A pencil sharpener

These are some of the shapes and drawing terms you need to know to draw Montana's sights and symbols:

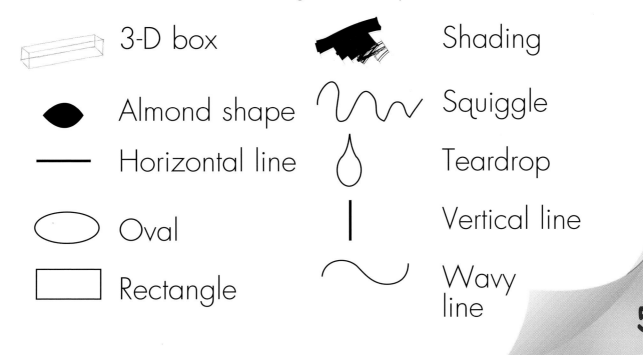

3-D box

Shading

Almond shape

Squiggle

Horizontal line

Teardrop

Oval

Vertical line

Rectangle

Wavy line

The Treasure State

The name Montana comes from the Spanish word for mountain, *montana*. In Spanish it is pronounced "mawn-TAN-ya." Montana is called the Treasure State because so many treasures can be found both below and above the ground in the state's 147,556 square miles (382,168 sq km) of land. Mining for gold and for silver is an important part of Montana's economic and cultural history. Gold mined from Virginia City in 1863 helped the Union win the Civil War. Mining is still a big industry today. In fact Montana has more sapphires than does any other U.S. state.

Montana's environment offers its own treasures. In northwest Montana, Flathead River boasts powerful white-water rapids. The glaciers in Glacier National Park are another natural wonder. In the south of the state, frozen grasshoppers can be seen in the ice of Grasshopper Glacier, near Cooke City, Montana. Nearby is the northeast entrance to Yellowstone National Park, the world's first national park.

Reynolds Mountain towers over the Logan Pass Visitor Center in Glacier National Park.

Artist in Montana

Charles Marion Russell

Charles Marion Russell is famous for his paintings and his sketches of American frontier cowboys and Native Americans. Russell was born in Saint Louis, Missouri, on March 19, 1864. During his childhood, he sketched images of cowboys and Native Americans. Russell dreamed of becoming a cowboy. At age 16, he left Missouri and went to Montana to become a sheepherder. Two years later, he was hired to be a cowboy. Russell spent many hours every day drawing what he saw around him, including wild animals, horses, cowboys, Native Americans, and the western landscape. By 1888, *Harper's*

Russell sometimes illustrated his letters with sketches like this one, entitled *Maney Snows Have Fallen.*

Weekly had published one of his sketches. His artistic talent and firsthand experience as a cowboy helped him to produce paintings and sketches that showed realistic images of the lives of cowboys and of Native Americans. Russell's paintings showed Native Americans as heroes, trying to keep settlers from taking away the land. This was not the common way to show Native Americans in the 1880s. By 1892, Russell was painting full-time. Sometimes he gave paintings as payment for the money he owed. Russell died in 1926, but he remains one of this country's most beloved painters of western life.

This painting, entitled *Indians Crossing the Plains*, measures 10 ¾" x 15" (27 cm x 38 cm).

Map of Montana

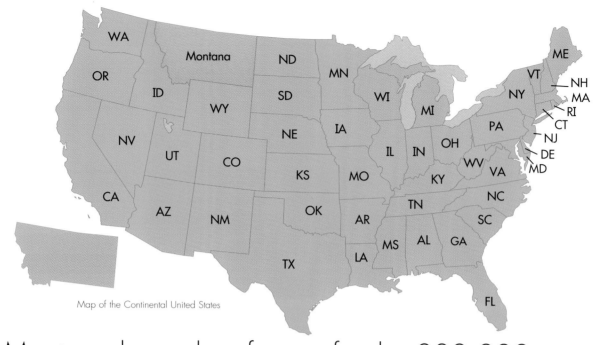

Map of the Continental United States

Montana has a lot of room for the 880,000 people who live in the state. Montana's most populated city is Billings, with about 91,200 residents. Twenty-eight thousand people live in the capital city, Helena. Montana is home to more than 50 peaks of the Rocky Mountains, known as the Rockies. Granite Peak is the tallest peak in the state, rising 12,799 feet (3,901 m) above sea level. Montana is known for its beautiful scenery, which includes the Rockies, Glacier National Park, and Flathead Lake. Prairies cover the eastern side of the state. Montana borders North Dakota, South Dakota, Wyoming, Idaho, and the Canadian provinces of British Columbia, Alberta, and Saskatchewan.

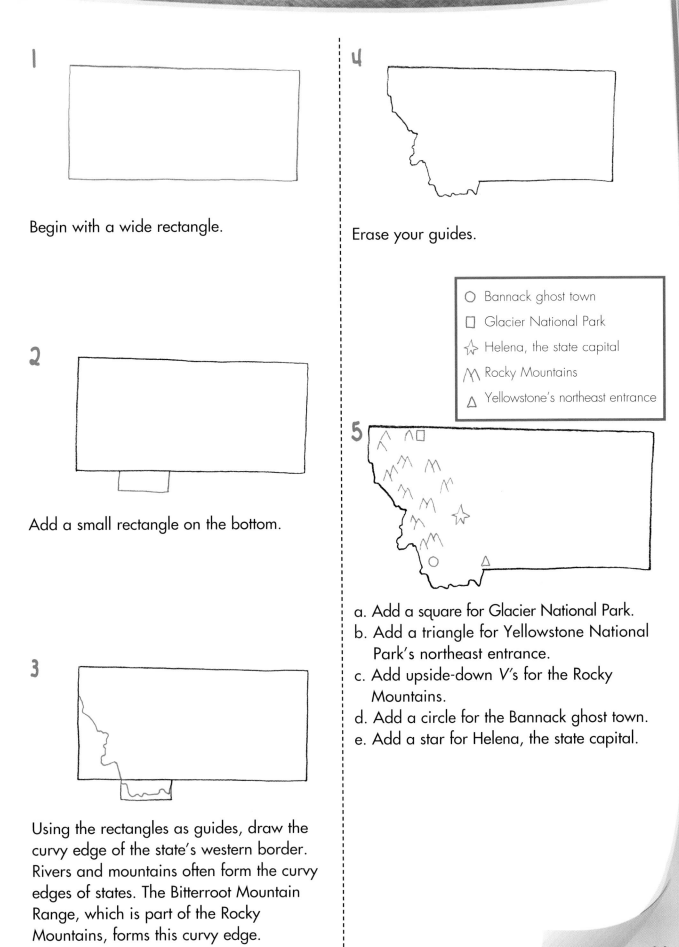

1

Begin with a wide rectangle.

2

Add a small rectangle on the bottom.

3

Using the rectangles as guides, draw the curvy edge of the state's western border. Rivers and mountains often form the curvy edges of states. The Bitterroot Mountain Range, which is part of the Rocky Mountains, forms this curvy edge.

4

Erase your guides.

○ Bannack ghost town
□ Glacier National Park
☆ Helena, the state capital
∧∧ Rocky Mountains
△ Yellowstone's northeast entrance

5

a. Add a square for Glacier National Park.
b. Add a triangle for Yellowstone National Park's northeast entrance.
c. Add upside-down V's for the Rocky Mountains.
d. Add a circle for the Bannack ghost town.
e. Add a star for Helena, the state capital.

The State Seal

The state seal of Montana was the seal of the Montana territory before Montana became a state in 1889. The seal was designed in 1865, and it became the official state seal in 1893. The plow, the pickax, and the shovel in the front of the image represent the frontier history of the state. The state motto, *oro y plata*, is Spanish for "gold and silver." This motto states the importance of mining to the state. Around the central image are the words "The Great Seal of the State of Montana." The state seal also highlights Montana's beautiful scenery, including mountains, waterfalls, rivers, trees, and plenty of sky.

1

Begin with a circle. Add clouds inside the circle, toward the top.

2

Add jagged mountains on the left side. Draw a cliff by drawing a crooked line diagonally across the circle and two short vertical lines.

3

On the right side, draw a jagged line for more mountains. Make a waterfall out of crooked rectangles. This waterfall is Great Falls. Make wavy lines to show the river.

4

Draw trees under the mountains on the left. Add some horizontal lines and a short vertical line to form another cliff and more ground.

5

Add the shovel and the pickax in the front of the seal. Notice how their handles cross over each other.

6

Add a plow behind the pickax and the shovel.

7

Make a banner at the bottom of the seal using curved lines.

8

Draw a bigger circle around your seal. Write in the words "THE GREAT SEAL OF THE STATE OF MONTANA." Shade your image.

13

The State Flag

The First Montana Infantry flew a flag during the Spanish-American War, a war between Spain and the United States that began in 1898. In 1905, that flag was officially adopted as the state flag. The first flag did not have the name "Montana" on it. In 1981, "Montana" was added in gold letters. The flag has a blue background. The image from the state seal is in the center of the flag. The Great Falls of the Missouri River and the river itself can be seen in the image's background. Mountains stand to the left of the river. The sun, a sign of promise and the future, is shown rising above the mountains.

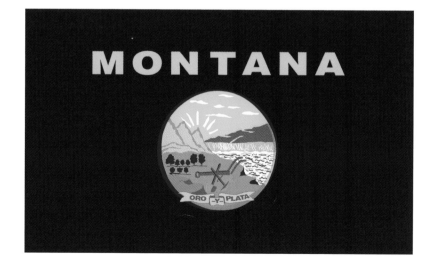

1

Begin with a rectangle.

2

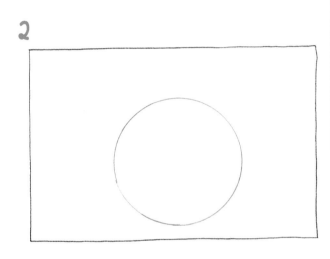

Make a circle in the rectangle's center.

3

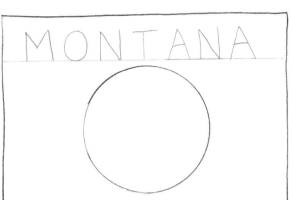

Draw a horizontal guideline above the circle. This will help you keep your letters straight as you write "MONTANA" along the line.

4

Erase the guideline. In the center of the circle add a smaller circle and then draw the image from the state seal. Do not include the words from the outer circle of the seal. The steps are shown on page 13.

The Bitterroot

On February 27, 1895, the bitterroot (*Lewisia rediviva*) was named Montana's official state flower. Meriwether Lewis, an early explorer of the American West, was the first European to discover the bitterroot. That is why Lewis's name is part of the flower's scientific name. The bitterroot has pink blossoms and grows close to the ground. It can live without water for more than a year. The flower is so popular that people in Montana have named the Bitterroot Mountain Range, the Bitterroot River, and the Bitter Root Valley after it! The flower's root was a favorite food for the Native Americans and the European settlers in the area. They boiled it and ate it with meat and berries.

1

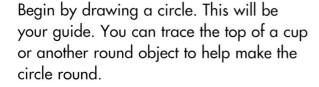

Begin by drawing a circle. This will be your guide. You can trace the top of a cup or another round object to help make the circle round.

2

Draw a small circle in the center of the first circle. This will be the center of the flower.

3

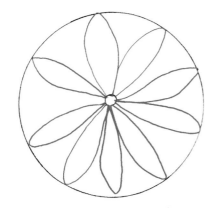

Draw long petals coming out of the center of the flower. Notice that no two petals are exactly alike. Some are thinner and some are thicker. Others may have been chewed by an insect.

4

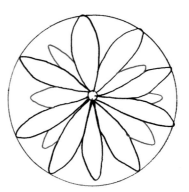

Fill in the flower by adding shorter petals that peek from behind the others.

5

Add stripes to the leaves by repeating a lot of thin lines.

6

Shade the edges of the petals. Notice that the petals are lightest in the center of the flower. Complete your flower by adding straight lines with shaded circles on the ends in the center of the flower.

The Ponderosa Pine

The ponderosa pine (*Pinus ponderosa*) is native to the Rocky Mountains and became the official state tree of Montana in 1949. The ponderosa pine has many other names, including the western yellow pine, the Montana black pine, the heavy-wooded pine, and the foothills yellow pine. It is a very large tree with dark brown, almost black, bark that is divided into ridges. The needles on the ponderosa pine are dark green and are clumped in groups of two or three. The tree has light-reddish-brown pinecones that are covered in prickly scales and measure 3 to 6 inches (8–15 cm) long.

1

Begin by drawing a tall, skinny triangle for the tree's trunk. Ponderosa pine trees can be 200 feet (61 m) tall, so you want the trunk to be long and thin.

2

Add thick branches and thin branches. You might want to use wavy lines, because the bark is rough and bumpy.

3

The ponderosa pine has a texture, or feel different from many other trees. It is made up of layers of curvy disks of bark. To draw that texture, you can use many layers of wavy lines.

4

The ponderosa pine branches are covered with thin, prickly needles. You can draw the texture of these needles by layering a lot of small, scratchy lines on top of one another. Add detail.

19

The Western Meadowlark

In 1931, Montana adopted the western meadowlark (*Sturnella neglecta*) as the official state bird. In 1805, explorer Meriwether Lewis first noted the western meadowlark in his journal. There are both eastern and western meadowlarks. As their name suggests, western meadowlarks live in the western United States. The two meadowlarks are hard to tell apart by sight, but their singing voices are different. The western meadowlark has a garbled song. The eastern meadowlark has a clear whistle. Both types have yellow bellies and black-and-brown-and-white-speckled backs. Adults have black *V*'s on their chests. Female meadowlarks lay about five white-and-brown, purple-spotted eggs once or twice a year.

1

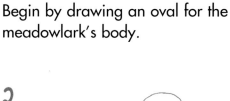

Begin by drawing an oval for the meadowlark's body.

2

Add a smaller oval for the head.

3

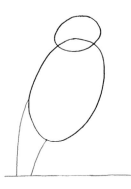

Draw a horizontal line below the bird. Make two curved lines between the body and the horizontal line for the bird's tail feathers.

4

Add the bird's small legs using two *U*-shaped lines and two pairs of straight lines.

5

Use curved triangle shapes to give the bird two small feet.

6

Add the beak by drawing the capital letter *M*. This meadowlark is singing. Its beak is open.

7

Redraw the shape of the bird as you erase the guides and extra lines. Add the eye.

8

Now add shading. Notice that the bird has spotted feathers.

Bannack, Montana

In July 1862, John White, of Colorado, traveled north with a group of men to search for gold. They set up camp on the east side of the Rocky Mountains by a creek that they named Grasshopper Creek, because there were so many grasshoppers there. Soon the men found gold, some of the first in the Montana area. More people came to "Grasshopper Diggins." By fall 1862, 400 people were living at the mining camp, called Bannack. By spring that number had swelled to 3,000. Bannack became Montana's first territorial capital. By the 1940s, the gold rush had ended, and most people had moved away. Bannack became a ghost town. Many of the original buildings remained, and Bannack was named a state park in 1954.

1

This ghost town is at the base of some hills. First use crooked lines to outline some tall hills in the background.

2

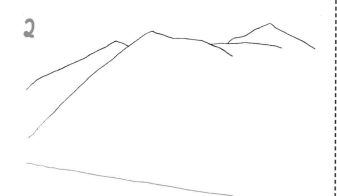

Add a diagonal line in front of the hills. This will be the road through the ghost town.

3

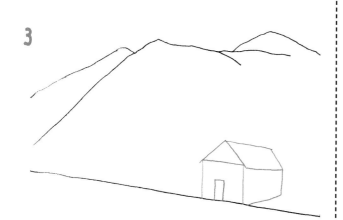

Draw a small house along the road. Start with a square, then add a triangle on top. Add a door. Make slanting rectangles for the roof and side of the house. It's okay if your lines aren't perfectly straight. Ghost town buildings are usually crooked, with chipped paint, broken boards, and cracked or missing windows.

4

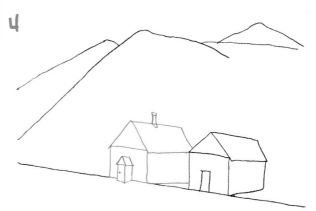

Add a second house. Use two slanted rectangles, a triangle, and a square. Add a chimney, a doorway, and a doorknob.

5

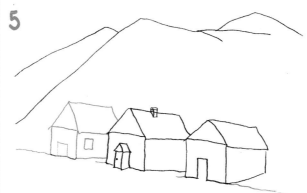

Add a third house. Then redraw your bottom line to make it look wavier. It's a dirt road, so it should look bumpy and irregular.

6

Shade your drawing. You can create the look of old, broken wood by repeating lines. Make darker lines for cracks in the wood. You can also add some tall grass along the road to make it look like no one uses it anymore.

The Rocky Mountains

The Rocky Mountains, or Rockies, cover more than 3,000 miles (4,828 km) of land. This mountain range starts in Colorado and extends through western Montana. The height of the range varies from 4,900 feet (1,493.5 m) to 14,516 feet (4,424 m) above sea level. The mountains began to form during the Cretaceous period, a time between 140 million and 65 million years ago. For at least the past 10,000 to 12,000 years, humans have lived in these mountains. They were home to ancient peoples, called Paleo-Indians, and to other Native Americans long before Lewis and Clark explored them in 1805. Today the Rocky Mountains attract millions of tourists every year.

1

Begin by drawing a rectangle for the border of your picture.

2

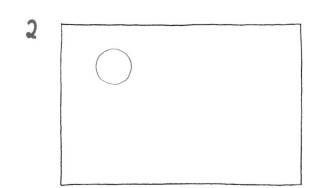

Draw a circle. That will be the moon over the mountains.

3

Next draw the edge of the mountains. You might want to use a jagged line, because the mountains are rocky and are covered with pine trees.

4

Draw a straight line across the lower part of your picture area. This is the place where the lake meets the mountains. Then outline a clump of trees on the right. They can be many different shapes, either short or tall.

5

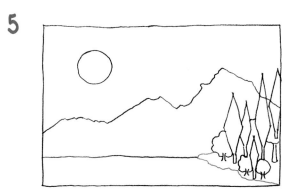

Next draw a crooked line to show the little island of land on which the trees are growing. It sticks out into the water.

6

Add leaves and pine needles to the trees by repeating both squiggly and straight lines. Shade the mountains so that they look dark against the sky. Draw wavy lines to make the lake look like water. Shade the sky lightly so that the moon is the brightest thing in your picture.

25

The Grizzly Bear

The grizzly bear (*Ursus arctos horribilis*), Montana's state animal, can be found in mountains throughout the state. Male grizzly bears usually weigh about 350 pounds (159 kg) but can weigh as much as 900 pounds (408 kg). Females are smaller. They weigh about 275 pounds (125 kg). When walking on all four legs, grizzly bears are about 3½ to 4 feet (1–1.2 m) tall, but when they stand on their two hind legs, they can be from 6 to 7 feet (1.8–2 m) tall. They have great senses of sight, of hearing, and of smell. Standing on their hind legs helps them to see, to hear, and to smell even better. Grizzly bears can run as fast as 35 miles per hour (56 km/h). They eat berries, roots, grasses, and animals, such as fish.

1

Draw a circle for the head and a smaller circle for the grizzly's shoulder.

2

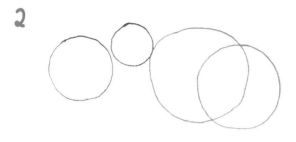

Add two more overlapping circles for the grizzly's belly and rear.

3

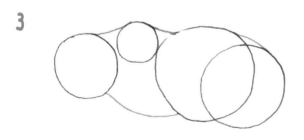

Join the circles with curved lines to make the top of the bear's head and back. Draw a curved line below the front circles to form the bear's belly.

4

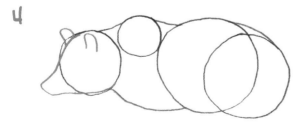

Add the grizzly's snout. The snout is the front part of the head, including the bear's nose, jaws, and mouth. Draw the bear's ears.

5

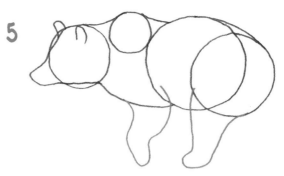

Draw the rounded shapes of the bear's front and rear legs.

6

Add legs on the other side of the bear.

7

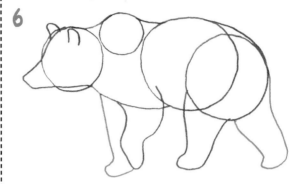

Add the bear's eye, nose, and mouth.

8

Erase your guides and shade. Make the bear look furry by repeating straight lines. Make some lines lighter on the bear's back and shoulders to show the sunlight on its fur.

Montana's Capitol

In 1894, Helena became Montana's capital city. One year later a nationwide competition was held to find an architect to design the state capitol building. George R. Mann from St. Louis, Missouri, won the competition. However another architect had to be hired because of a governmental mistake. In 1898, the Iowan team of Charles Bell and John Kent began designing the capitol. The cornerstone of the capitol building was laid on July 4, 1899. Exactly three years later, on July 4, 1902, there was a ceremony to dedicate the building. The building's east and west wings were added between 1909 and 1912. On top of the capitol building stands a large, copper dome.

1

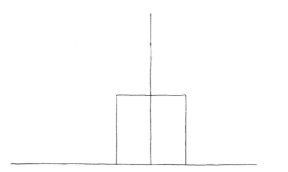

Draw a horizontal line. Add a vertical line from the top of the page to the center of the first line. Draw a square on these guides.

2

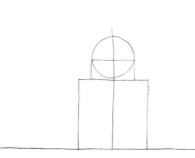

Draw a rectangle on top of the square. Add a circle, half in and half out of the rectangle. The circle will help you make the dome.

3

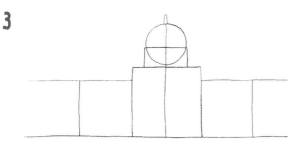

You can use a small finger shape to represent the statue on top of the dome. Add two boxes on each side of the square.

4

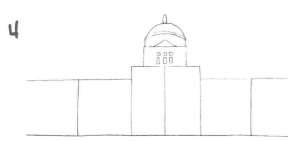

Erase extra lines. Add details to the dome. These include rectangles for windows, a triangle, and horizontal bands across the dome.

5

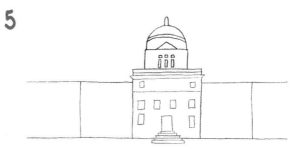

Add more windows and a doorway. Make stairs using skinny rectangles. Add detail.

6

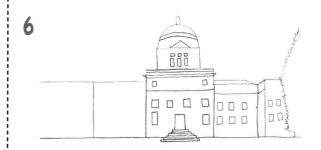

Draw windows on the right side. Add vertical and horizontal lines to the side of the building. Draw a pine tree. Erase any extra lines.

7

Repeat step 6 on the left side. Make your pine trees with jagged lines. Add detail. Erase any extra lines.

8

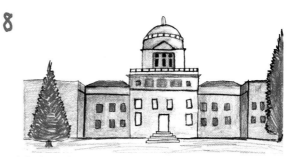

Add detail and shading to the capitol.

Montana State Facts

Statehood	November 8, 1889, 41st state
Area	147,556 square miles (382,168 sq km)
Population	880,000
Capital	Helena, population, 28,000
Most Populated City	Billings, population, 91,200
Industries	Tourism, forest products, food processing, mining, construction
Agriculture	Dairy products, wheat, cattle, hay, barley, sugar beets
Animal	Grizzly bear
Bird	Western meadowlark
Flower	Bitterroot
Fish	Blackspotted cutthroat trout
Fossil	Duck-billed dinosaur
Tree	Ponderosa pine
Gemstones	Sapphire and agate
Grass	Bluebunch wheatgrass
Motto	*Oro y plata*, or Gold And Silver
Arboretum	University of Montana, Missoula
Vietnam Veterans' Memorial	Stoddard Park, Butte, Montana
Nickname	The Treasure State

Glossary

adopted (uh-DPOPT-ed) To have accepted or approved something.

agriculture (A-grih-kul-cher) Having to do with farms or farming.

ancient (AYN-chent) Very old; from a long time ago.

architect (AR-kih-tekt) Someone who designs buildings.

ceremony (SEHR-ih-moh-nee) A series of acts done on a special occasion.

competition (kom-pih-TIH-shin) A contest to see who is the best at something.

cornerstone (KOR-nur-stohn) The first, usually large, stone placed when building a building.

dedicate (DEH-dih-kayt) To devote to a purpose.

environment (en-VY-urn-ment) All the living things and conditions that make up a place.

garbled (GAR-buld) Unclear or mixed up.

glaciers (GLAY-shurz) Large masses of ice in very cold regions or on the tops of high mountains.

industry (IN-dus-tree) A system of work, or labor.

infantry (IN-fuhn-tree) A group of men in the military.

Louisiana Purchase. (loo-EE-zee-a-nuh PER-ches) Land that the United States bought from France in 1803 that included the present state of Montana.

sapphires (SA-fyrz) Precious stones that are blue in color.

Index

Web Sites

To learn more about Montana, check out this Web site:
www.montanakids.com